To J. A. B.
C. B.

To my niece Eleonora
and my nephew Alessandro
L. G.

First published 2011 by Walker Books Ltd
87 Vauxhall Walk, London SE11 5HJ

2 4 6 8 10 9 7 5 3 1

Text © 2011 Chris Butterworth
Illustrations © 2011 Lucia Gaggiotti

The right of Chris Butterworth and Lucia Gaggiotti to be identified as author and illustrator
respectively of this work has been asserted by them in accordance with the Copyright,
Designs and Patents Act 1988

This book has been typeset in VAG Rounded

Printed in China

British Library Cataloguing in Publication Data:
a catalogue record for this book is available from the British Library

ISBN 978-1-4063-1090-0

www.walker.co.uk

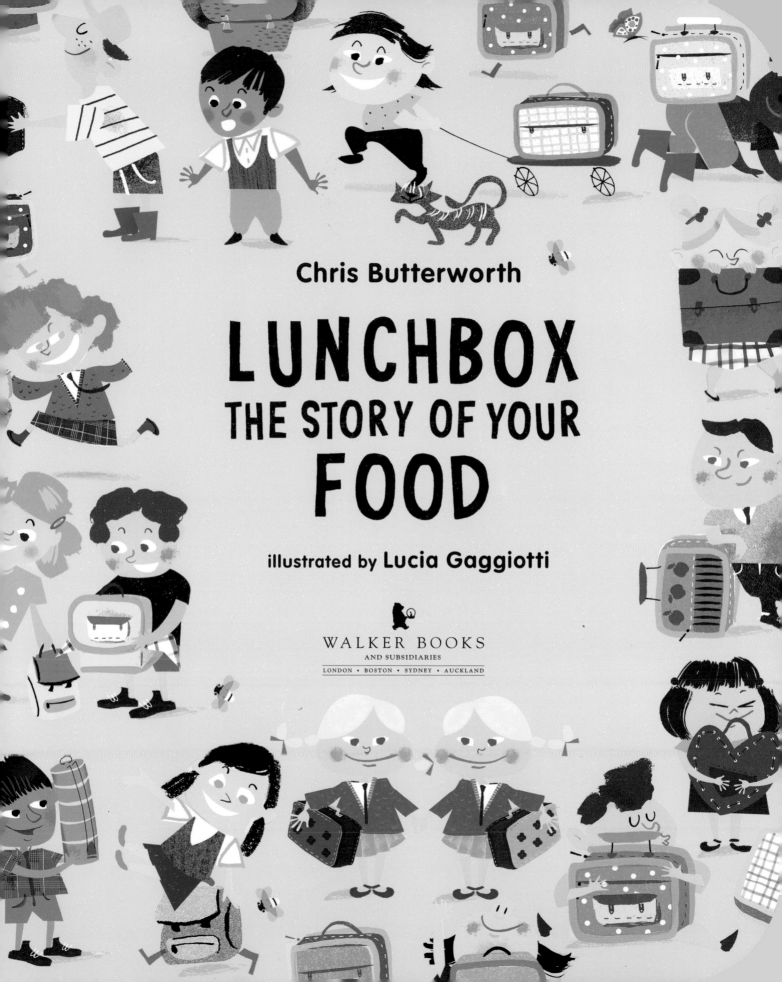

Chris Butterworth

LUNCHBOX
THE STORY OF YOUR
FOOD

illustrated by **Lucia Gaggiotti**

WALKER BOOKS
AND SUBSIDIARIES
LONDON · BOSTON · SYDNEY · AUCKLAND

ONE of the best bits of the day is when you lift the lid of your lunchbox to see what's inside. Your mum or your dad has packed it with lots of tasty things to eat. They probably got all the food from a shop – but food doesn't grow in shops!

So where did it come from before it was in the shop?

Just how **DiD** all this food get in your lunchbox?

HOW DiD THE **BREAD** iN YOUR SANDWiCH GET iN YOUR LUNCHBOX?

A farmer planted seeds in spring and by summer they'd grown into tall, waving wheat with fat, ripe grains at the tip of every stalk.

The farmer cut the wheat with a giant combine harvester, and sent it to a flour mill.

GRAINS

The miller ground the grains into flour, and trucks took the flour to a bakery.

The baker mixed the flour with water, sugar and yeast, kneaded it into a soft, squashy dough, and baked it in a very hot oven.

YEAST

SUGAR

WATER

FLOUR

Out came fresh loaves of bread – ready to send to the shops.

Take a bite of the bread in your sandwich – **MMMMMM**, crusty on the outside and soft in the middle!

HOW DiD THE CHEESE iN YOUR SANDWiCH GET iN YOUR LUNCHBOX?

Your cheese was once milk that came from a cow. A farmer milked the cows, and a tanker from the dairy came to collect the milk.

1. In the dairy, cheesemakers warmed up the milk …

2. … and added bacteria to make it turn sour and thick.

5. They drained off the whey, chopped up the rubbery curds, added some salt, and pressed them into blocks.

3. Then they added stuff called rennet and it changed again ...

4. ... into bits of curd, floating in whey.

6. They stored the blocks for months until the cheese was ripe.

Bite into your cheese. It's creamy and smooth, but tasty too – and **TiNGLY** on your tongue!

13

HOW DiD YOUR **TOMATOES** GET iN YOUR LUNCHBOX?

Last summer, your tomatoes were growing in a big plastic tunnel full of tomato plants.

The sun and the warmth made the plants grow tall and bloom with yellow flowers. As each flower died, a tiny green tomato fruit began to grow from its middle.

Day by day, the plants sucked up water and the tomatoes swelled from green to orange to red.

When bunches of ripe scarlet tomatoes dangled from the branches, the grower picked them ...

1. ... sorted them ...

2. ... packed them ...

3. ... and sent them to the shops.

POP one in your mouth and squish the sweet-sour juice out!

HOW DiD YOUR APPLE JUiCE GET iN YOUR LUNCHBOX?

Last spring, the apple trees in the orchard were full of flowers. In summer, tiny apple buds grew from each flower stalk. The buds kept growing, and by autumn the trees were full of ripe, sweet fruit.

Gangs of pickers climbed into the trees, and filled their bins with fruit.

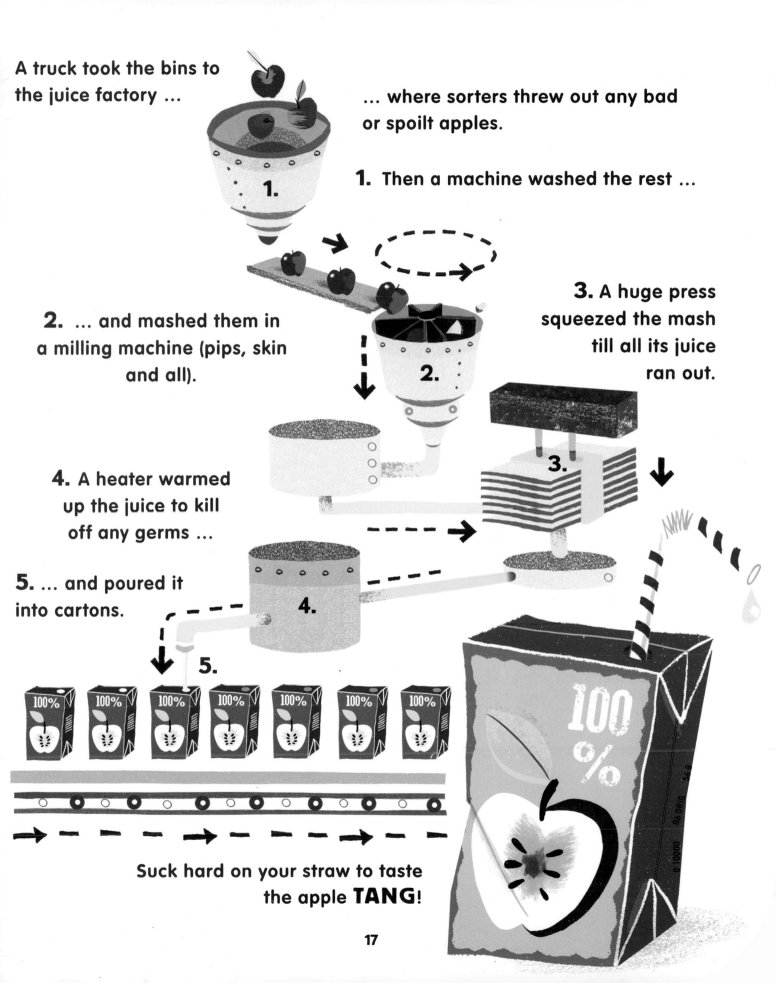

A truck took the bins to the juice factory ...

... where sorters threw out any bad or spoilt apples.

1. Then a machine washed the rest ...

2. ... and mashed them in a milling machine (pips, skin and all).

3. A huge press squeezed the mash till all its juice ran out.

4. A heater warmed up the juice to kill off any germs ...

5. ... and poured it into cartons.

Suck hard on your straw to taste the apple **TANG!**

100%

HOW DiD YOUR **CARROTS** GET iN YOUR LUNCHBOX?

Last spring, your carrots were growing in a field on a vegetable farm. You wouldn't have seen any carrots then, just long rows of feathery leaves.

As the leaves grew taller in the summer sun, each carrot root pushed deeper into the earth, soaking up water and turning orange. By late summer, they had swelled so much that the top of each carrot poked out of the earth.

Pickers pulled them up.

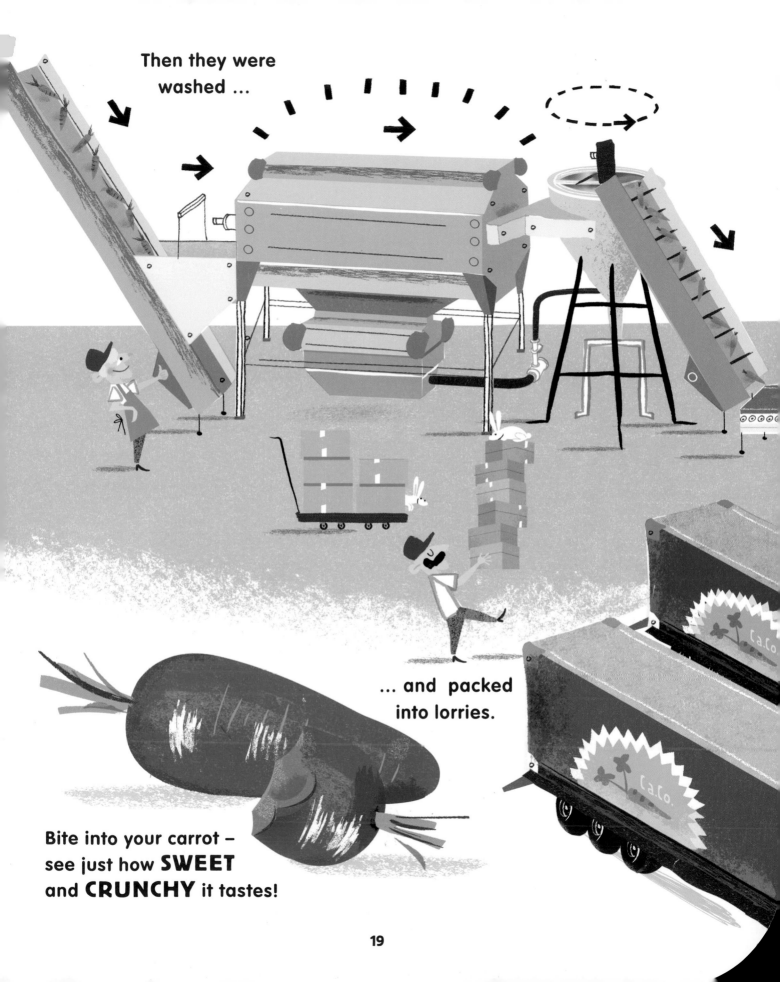

Then they were washed ...

... and packed into lorries.

Bite into your carrot – see just how **SWEET** and **CRUNCHY** it tastes!

19

HOW DiD THE CHOCOLATE CHiP iN YOUR BiSCUiT GET iNTO YOUR LUNCHBOX?

Biscuits are made from flour, sugar and butter – and this one's got chocolate chips in it.

Chocolate starts off as a bean – well, lots of beans – which grow in pods on a cocoa tree.

The pods are picked from the tree. Then they're cut open and the beans are scooped out. These beans are spread out and left to dry in the sun.

The dried beans are taken to a factory – sometimes on the other side of the world.

In the factory, they're cleaned then … **1.** roasted …

2. … and ground to a thick sticky paste.

3. Sugar's mixed in, so the paste gets sweeter, but it's still gritty, so it's squeezed, stirred, melted and cooled …

1.

2. →

3.

… to make it really smooooooth (it takes a lot of work to make chocolate!).

4. Finally the chocolate is moulded into blocks.

4.

3578912

These are made into little chips that will **MELT** in your mouth all over again!

HOW DiD YOUR CLEMENTiNE GET iN YOUR LUNCHBOX?

Your clementine is a kind of berry, and it grew on a tree. Early in summer, the trees in the clementine grove were full of sweet-smelling, waxy flowers.

As the flowers died, a tiny green clementine berry began to grow out of each one.

The clementines swelled in the warm sun, turning from green to yellow. By the time cooler winter weather arrived, the clementines had turned orange, and were so heavy and full of juice that they made the branches droop.

Pickers climbed ladders to reach them – they had to wear gloves so they didn't bruise the tender fruit inside the skin.

They washed them and packed them, and the grower sent the boxes in trucks to the market.

It's easy to peel a clementine! Then all you have to do is pop the **JUiCY** pieces in your mouth and bite: you won't find a single pip in it!

You've eaten it all – from the first bite of bread to the last piece of fruit! It came from fields and farms, from orchards, from groves and from dairies. So many people helped bring it to you – farmers and bakers, cheese-makers and chocolate-makers, pickers, packers and truck-drivers. And now it's all in your stomach, starting to do the job that food does ...

helping you grow taller and stronger, and giving you get-up-and-go!

You need more than lunch to make you grow and keep you healthy. Every day you need to choose food from each of the sections on this plate, and most of it should come from the "fruit and vegetables" and "carbohydrates" sections.

CARBOHYDRATES
These foods fill you up fast and give you the energy to keep going.

FRUiT and **VEGETABLES**
Your body needs lots of these to keep you healthy.

100%

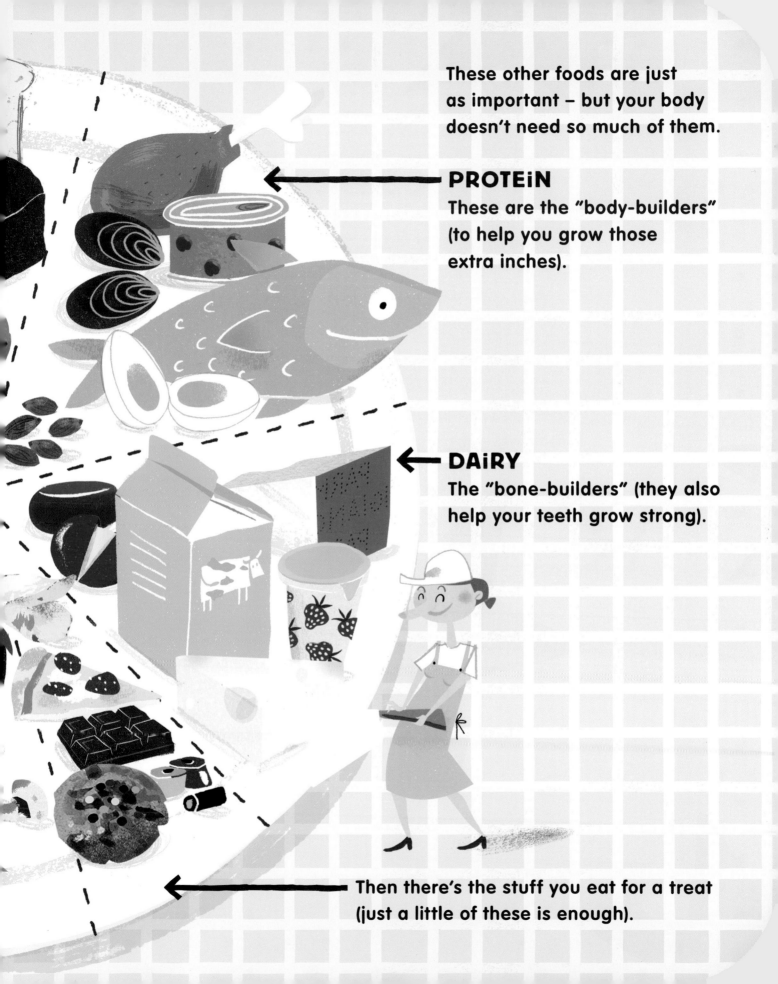

These other foods are just as important – but your body doesn't need so much of them.

PROTEiN
These are the "body-builders" (to help you grow those extra inches).

DAiRY
The "bone-builders" (they also help your teeth grow strong).

Then there's the stuff you eat for a treat (just a little of these is enough).

FOOD FACTS

Your body is mostly made of water, so you need about six drinks a day to keep topped up. Most of these drinks should be water (not fizzy pop, which has lots of sugar in it).

Your body is growing all the time (even when you're asleep!). So remember, don't skip breakfast – it gets your body through the day.

Too much sitting about won't keep your body fit. It doesn't matter if you chase a ball, your dog, or your friends – but spend about an hour a day on the move!

It's good to eat five different kinds of fruit and vegetables every day. Why not try a new one this week?

iNDEX